TRAGEDY
IN
HAPPY VALLEY

Audrey Rodgers

Cover artwork by Kaye Productions

Published by Kaye Productions

www.kayeproductions.com

ISBN 978-0-9829716-5-9

PRINTED IN THE UNITED STATES OF AMERICA

1 3 5 7 9 10 8 6 4 2

First Edition

Acknowledgements

*Grateful thanks to David and Candy
Kaye for their generous help in the
creation of this book. In addition, I am
deeply indebted to Amy Sinenta whose
intelligence, sensitivity, and persistence
made this a pleasurable endeavor.*

foreword

AND THIS TOO SHALL PASS.....

Table Of Contents

TRAGEDY
IN
HAPPY VALLEY

INTRODUCTION

It is with great humility that I write of the suffering, shame, pride, and regret that threatened the very existence of Penn State University and "Happy Valley" Pennsylvania. I was there, and the shock and sadness will live with me for all time. And so my story is part of Happy Valley's story and the pain is understandably my pain as is the hoped for recovery.

I would go backward in time to the year 1950 when two excited instructors were headed for the picturesque center of Pennsylvania—our Doctorates clutched in our hands, our hopes high, our future unknown. We were city bred and were yet to learn what life would be like "far from the madding crowd." Entering Centre County, we were touched by the bucolic flavor of the place, but soon this was dispelled by the breath-taking beauty of the University Campus. We had no inkling that a malevolent wind would sweep the landscape magic and ultimately stun the world in 2011.

There at our feet, was The Pennsylvania State University—Academic Paradiso. We had little money, a three-year old son, and a used Plymouth car. We could not afford a town apartment so we settled for a small house on a stream in nearby Lemont and a beautiful, gentle, golden Collie we named "Lassie." We were soon to forget the grinding hustle and bustle of the city and became captivated by the rural atmosphere— peaceful, beautiful, and comfortable.

Life in Happy Valley, as it came to be known, became a succession of beginnings—beginnings of friendship, beginnings of advanced learning, beginnings of serious research, and beginnings of the joy of achievement. Though our families were miles away, we centered our hopes on personal accomplishment. Study was foremost, but so was bridge, football Saturdays, the movies, and weekly dinners at the Tavern. We were both extroverts and cherished good company and good conversation. Thus, we made friends who are still in touch.

Teaching was our love. My husband quickly found warm colleagues in the Department of Geography and I studied and taught in the English Department, finding others whose interests echoed my own. In a word we were happy, though we never dwelled on our good fortune or discussed the idyllic life—this was the path we had chosen and we envisioned no other.

Every seven years we were awarded a sabbatical leave with the option of twelve months at half pay or six months at full pay. This was manna from heaven for a Geographer or any professor who wished to complete research in another field of his or her specialty. I used the time abroad to teach English for the U.S. State Department and to write research essays on American poets Emily Dickinson and T.S. Eliot. As exciting as Italy, France, and China were, I longed to return to the tranquil world of Happy Valley. Yet I still hold in my heart a special place for the hills of Roma and the beauty of the Italian language. Yes, you can go home again, and we did.

Yet peace and contentment rarely last for long and our tranquil life was shattered by the Penn State Scandal. Though never involved in the tumultuous events that grew with each discovery, our world was struck not to return for three years.

TRAGEDY IN HAPPY VALLEY

On a warm Autumn morning The Pennsylvania State University fell from Grace. Long heralded as a champion of college football, a promoter of Academic standards. a model for students, faculty, and retirees, Penn State boasted a stellar position in the hierarchy of advanced institutions. Then, the scandal that threatened the University and shocked the country from coast to coast left an unbelieving State College population stunned by the unfolding "revelations" that would come to be known as the "Sandusky Scandal". It had all the trappings of a Greek tragedy. In recent times, no crime has shaken the American heartland as this.

My purpose here is not to seek blame, nor to cite all state universities as breeding grounds for aberrational behavior. Rather I aim to reach the State University world—the "hallowed" ground that boasts good and harbors evil.

My aim, first and foremost, is to anatomize the national State college internal structures—surprisingly similar countrywide—despite variations we can ascribe to historical events. As we penetrate college after college, there was little to differentiate one from another. Instead both in academics and organizational hierarchy there was a remarkable similarity.

Given this "background" I will enter the world of The Pennsylvania State University, commonly referred to as Penn State or PSU. Its distinct departure from its sisterhood—where it is a part of the state university system and where it is different.

I offer my own experience at Penn State—as both graduate student and ultimately as Professor Emerita. After thirty-eight years of teaching there, I have gained some insight—not about the "Greek Tragedy" we have recently witnessed—but of the depth of the suffering and the need for—as Italians would say—*Anima e Cuore*.

What follows is the true story. It happened where it was least expected to happen. It happened in rural America—"far from the Madding crowd".,. It happened at the highest level of man's intellectual achievement. It happened at Penn State. And it almost destroyed the respectable

6

reputation of a small home town—State College. It was known as The Sandusky Scandal. Sheltered by the Seven Mountains, Penn State was often proudly referred to as the safest campus in America.

Fall Foliage in the Valley[1]

No train stopped here; few planes touch down on its landing sites; and roaming theatres were infrequent. This does not suggest that Penn State was in any way, bucolic. Complex, sophisticated, au courant with the world at large, the University lived up to the pride its students revealed.

---

1 Courtesy of Central Pennsylvania Convention and Visitors Bureau

Yet tragedy befell Happy Valley and its mystery will remain for many years complex , unforeseen, and all but insoluble. The "innocent" will suffer as they have these past three years. The "guilty" will trek from court to court claiming their innocence while the Public grows increasingly more confused.

Alumni Center[1]

Hints of Spring are in the air. The early Forsythia are crowding the Mall. The scent of Lilac fills our heads. Hope cancels despair. State College and the University are fighting their way back to their cherished normalcy. And we will overcome. We will take the Rose Bowl. We will

---

1 Courtesy of Central Pennsylvania Convention and Visitors Bureau

live to see our children and our grandchildren sing out **WE ARE PENN STATE** again.

Penn State's mascot, the Nittany Lion[1]

1 Courtesy of Central Pennsylvania Convention and Visitors Bureau

Chapter I

THE STATE UNIVERSITY

Most State Universities look remarkably similar in appearance. They had been constructed on broad, beautiful grounds that did not attract the bustling, fast-paced tempo of a growing America. In fact, the typical State University,

Aerial View of Old Main¹

---

1 Courtesy of Central Pennsylvania Convention and Visitors Bureau

from its inception, prided itself on its isolation from the hustle- bustle of the stock market, from the usual "influence for success, and from the emphasis on equating advancement with money. Most State Universities exulted in being "Far from the madding crowd."

Into these bucolic towns the founding fathers of the State University established their academic dreams on a picturesque campus framed by stately buildings. And side by side the former "small town" was to gain America's respect.

Old Main in the summer[1]

To add to their importance, most of the universities became surrounded with small, highly technical research centers—more attractive to the world—a model for raising children, prospering financially, and offering a pleasurable environment even as their university grew in stature, in size, in the fruits of campus progress in little known research. It was a remarkable first step in scientific cooperation and discovery.

Elms line the Mall[1]

But the sheer beauty of these university campuses was a universal quality. Most boasted a long Mall, lined with stately elm or oak or willow trees and interspersed with flowering gardens and brick or stone academic buildings.

The builders of all America's State Universities knew that knowledge and esthetics created a harmonious union and students were sensitive to their environment no matter the season. As for Faculty and Staff members, the physical beauty

---

1 Used with permission from PENN STATE | NEWS

of their university was a major element in their lives. The stroll to the next class was a welcome respite as the mammoth clock atop the formidable administrative building struck the hour.

View from College Avenue[1]

The history behind the creation of individual buildings reflects the disciplinary emphasis placed on each college so that every campus structure was known by its field of specialization.

Thus, as the years passed, the College of Science or Agriculture or Liberal Arts or Physical Education or Earth Science or Engineering were created, each proudly commanding its

1 Courtesy of Central Pennsylvania Convention and Visitors Bureau

own organization, its own administrative and educational standards, its own reputation. Like sentinels, each college both protected and maintained its integrity in a highly diversified arena—the University. There was much competition: for funds, for publicity, for advancement, and for "fame."

Old Main[1]

Inside each structure, a hierarchy of importance is maintained. The Dean is the most influential figure in all critical matters: hiring of faculty, promotions, salary, student concerns, and standards. Heads of Departments exercise the second most critical decision-making position,

---

1 Courtesy of Central Pennsylvania Convention and Visitors Bureau

although senior faculty exert a strong influence in hiring, firing, and promotion.

Any department in a state university could contain several individualized specialties. For example, Liberal Arts is the home for the Departments of French, English. German, and Classics in all state universities. All exercise a great deal of autonomy and strongly influence the Dean on matters of promotion and salary.

These unspoken influences are, at times, cause for friction between departments and lead to campus politics. Yet each state university maintains its strength, due largely to its relationship with the state legislature, for it is finally the legislature that controls the leadership and finances, and when in crisis the university acts as one.

What the Departments do not control, though a strong Head wields considerable power, is the University Calendar or the annual State University budget, or radical decisions such as expansion or the creation of new departments. These also are considerable sources of discontent among faculty members.

All this would suggest that I have disregarded the key factor—the students. I would emphasize that all the planning and execution of administrative matters in Academe must keep in mind the ultimate benefit for the student. Never let it be assumed that the chief objective of all state universities is to supply a comfortable ambiance for the research scholar's advancement in his field; the first priority is the student.

The Mall as Spring approaches[1]

The success in his career will rest on the quality of the knowledge he has gained in his four years or more at his university and the degree he has taken to learn. It is true that not all state universities hew to the highest standards, but it is here that the individual Department can demand the strictest goals. As the student begins the uphill climb from Freshman to Sophomore

1 Used with permission from PENN STATE | NEWS

to Junior to Senior he comes to understand that teaching and learning are his and his Professor's fundamental objectives.

Graduate study is another option for the students. It is here that he contemplates a particular career. Classes consist of six to ten students in a seminar room with less of an undergraduate atmosphere. Only senior faculty teach seminars.

The Penn State Nittany Lion[1]

But male students often apply for State Universities lured by the vision of four years of "foot-loose and fancy free." They dream of entering a fraternity or sorority and launch on a

1 Courtesy of Central Pennsylvania Convention and Visitors Bureau

dizzy climb of parties, liquor, football weekends, and ravishing girls. The other side of this fantasy is the female students who are frankly husband-hunting or at the very least, looking for a new romance. The center for all this day-dreaming is the Fraternity—long famous as the social locus for making dreams come true. Generally, Frats maintain a respectable reputation, but too often we hear of drinking, wild parties, too much sexual activity, too much fun and not enough studying. Executives have been successful in this "walk on the wild side" but with diligence and good common sense. Nonetheless, this problem haunts those who govern young, State University students and largely at the state's expense!

Walking between classes on a cool Fall day

This above all: it is a given that handsome scholarships and fellowships are more publicized and are more abundant in the private, ivy-league universities—Yale, Princeton and Harvard—given by grateful alumni who owe their success at the mere mention of their alma mater. Yet, state universities promise larger awards in aid to a far larger number of recipients than the Ivy. Another one of Democracy's triumphs.

Chapter II

BEFORE THE CRISIS

Penn State's beginnings were humble and attracted scant attention nationwide. It opened with the aid of a Land Grant and State support in 1859 as the Farmers' High School and expanded in 1862 as The Agricultural College of Pennsylvania.

Old Main - Farmers High School - 1859[1]

---

1 Used with permission from the Pennsylvania State University Library Archive Collection

Old Main and surrounding buildings - 1890[1]

Clearly, the institution had crossed the educational line into Academia. Twelve years later, this rural institution had grown in stature as The Pennsylvania State College. It became a university in 1953 with the proud name: The Pennsylvania State University. There, at the foot of the Seven Mountains—far from the madding crowd—Penn State would carve its future as one of America's outstanding educational centers.

Against the shimmering elms along the Mall and the rolling sweep of green lawn meeting the horizon in the distance, inside the brick and stone sentinels Professors conduct the business

---

1 Used with permission from the Pennsylvania State University Library Archive Collection

of educating America's young. At the peak of the Mall the Library dominates the landscape—a stately and stern reminder of the University's mission.

Paterno Patee Library[1]

The backbone of each College is, of course, the individual Department with its unique organization, power, and educational hiring aspects. For example, the College of Liberal Arts is the "home" for the Departments of English Literature and Creative Writing, French, Spanish, Italian, German, as well as Women's' Studies, American Studies, Psychology, Sociology. Economics and Speech.

1 Courtesy of Central Pennsylvania Convention and Visitors Bureau

The College of Earth and Mineral Sciences is the host for the Departments of Geography, Geology, as well as all advanced research and teaching of the many aspects of Mineral Sciences. One of the more revolutionary academic facets to have developed at Penn State is the adoption of Inter-disciplinary research and teaching. A Professor in one specialty now may find it productive to CROSS OVER to Political Science to investigate and produce rich results with the ideas and knowledge of a Political Science professor. This development has proven to be a formidable change not only in basic research but in the job market as well! The new Ph. D , knows more and offers more than other candidates.

Another important introduction adding to Penn State's luster was the STAR program adopted by every Department on campus. Essentially, national and international scholars were invited to Penn State as permanent faculty. Several faculty members of Penn State who had distinguished themselves as important scholars were chosen to become STAR professors. Thus, Dr. Herschel Leibowitz in Psychology was one such recipient as was Dr. Wulbur Zelinsky in Geography.

The award was handsome: those awarded were encouraged to continue their research—teaching and advising students was not obligatory although most of the STAR faculty did voluntarily teach and many coordinated their research with graduate students. It was a fortuitous program in bringing student and faculty of distinction together.

If all this emphasis upon academics suggests that all work and no play awaits the Penn State student. Let me emphasize that extra-curricular activities are in abundance here. Few universities in the United States could boast the great variety of opportunities for the student to escape the pressures of study.

Dance maraTHON[1]

---

1 Courtesy of Central Pennsylvania Convention and Visitors Bureau

There are social Clubs for virtually every discipline, but there are almost countless places students may seek to relax. The University offers both indoor 'and outdoor swimming pools, an indoor all-season ice-skating arena, tennis courts, practice fields for the aspiring football hopefuls, and—best of all—the Creamery which produces superb ice cream, cheeses, and snacks for the early morning hunger.

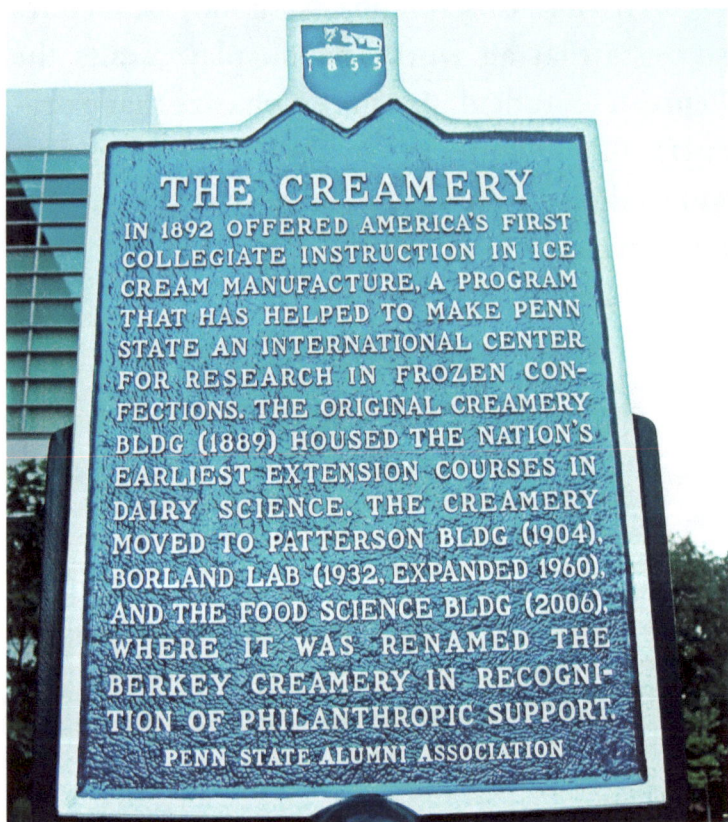

THE CREAMERY

IN 1892 OFFERED AMERICA'S FIRST COLLEGIATE INSTRUCTION IN ICE CREAM MANUFACTURE, A PROGRAM THAT HAS HELPED TO MAKE PENN STATE AN INTERNATIONAL CENTER FOR RESEARCH IN FROZEN CONFECTIONS. THE ORIGINAL CREAMERY BLDG (1889) HOUSED THE NATION'S EARLIEST EXTENSION COURSES IN DAIRY SCIENCE. THE CREAMERY MOVED TO PATTERSON BLDG (1904), BORLAND LAB (1932, EXPANDED 1960), AND THE FOOD SCIENCE BLDG (2006), WHERE IT WAS RENAMED THE BERKEY CREAMERY IN RECOGNITION OF PHILANTHROPIC SUPPORT.

PENN STATE ALUMNI ASSOCIATION

On a grander scale, Penn State conducts a year-round series of imported stars who perform plays, musicals, concerts—all open to University as well as State College residents. I would be amiss if I did not mention the Hub where clubs meet and where students drop in for a little relaxation.

But no activity can equal THE BIG THREE in popularity: Fraternity, Sorority, and—at the peak—Football. In actuality. All three are intimately related. Fraternity is every male student's dream. If selected during the "Rush," period. he is treated like a king and once a member, he is a Brother for life. All manner of pleasure awaits him: weekly "socials" with sororities complete with "drinking", dancing, and the effortless occupation of choosing from a bevy of girls. Needless to say, at times the drinking gets out of hand or the special date for the future belongs to another brother. With sensible management by the senior oversees parties need not be uncontrollable and can be tastefully handled by wiser heads. Above all, the fraternities do not wish to suffer a bad reputation or possible expulsion. Too many state universities have wrestled with drinking problems but administrations, cognizant of growing college costs are joining the universities to curb this dilemma.

Sorority is a much more tractable organization. Although now and then gossip reports a torrid love affair with a fraternity "Romeo," there is a general, humorous slant to these accounts as the Sisters play the field and enjoy a full social calendar. The Sisters study hard, spend long hours in the Library, and know that this is the only route to a good job. They enjoy the parties, are sensibly aware of Fraternity men, and genuinely enjoy the company of sorority Sisters. Less athletic than Frat Men, the Sisters take full advantage of ice-skating, tennis, volleyball, and swimming, as well as the Theatre productions, concerts, and "hen" parties.

All in all, the Fraternity/Sorority system is highly successful—students enjoy help in their studies from experienced upper class men and sound advice on the social scene. Lifetime friendships are formed and memories of life at Penn State held dear.

One could say that the town, the entire University, and perhaps the entire State are possessed with football fever from late August to New Year's Day. There is no way to describe the heightened sense of anticipation as the pre-game Blue-White Game.

Beaver Stadium[1]

The Nittany Lion at half-time[2]

1 Courtesy of Central Pennsylvania Convention and Visitors Bureau
2 Courtesy of Central Pennsylvania Convention and Visitors Bureau

Beaver Field in 1890[1]

Beaver Field - Penn State versus Pitt in 1966[2]

1 Used with permission from the Pennsylvania State University Library Archive Collection
2 Used with permission from the Pennsylvania State University Library Archive Collection

VICTORY RIOT BEAVER STADIUM
AFTER STATE BEAT N.C. STATE 13-8

Fans celebrate at Beaver Stadium [1]

There is no question that the star attraction of this University, hidden away in a valley of the Alleghenies, is Football. It would move prospective students to apply for admission a year in advance. During the long football season State College bustles with motel reservations; gift shops do an overwhelming business; restaurants

1 Used with permission from the Pennsylvania State University Library Archive Collection

buzz with speculation about the quarterback--the main topic of conversation among fans. Opening kick¬off signals the popular shout: WE ARE PENN STATE; joined with Joe Paterno's famous pacing; and the excitement awaiting them on the field. Other sports bring fans to their feet, but nothing can replace Penn State's enthusiasm when football season starts.

Penn State versus Temple[1]

Yes, there is violence, but it is carefully monitored by the players and coaches. Both players and fans have denounced unnecessary violence on the field and games and practice sessions have hewed to the standard of fair play. In its history since the Farmers High School Penn State has set an exemplary record. It is with

1 Courtesy of Central Pennsylvania Convention and Visitors Bureau

a sense of horror that the fans and indeed the country that recent events have tarnished Penn State's honorable reputation.

The excitement of football...[1]

America's long history of violence has been tumultuous: first, the battles of the American Revolution; then The Civil War; Two World Wars; and then Vietnam. And still she moved on to peace, survival and prosperity. We buried our dead and moved on to acceptance of past deeds. Little in life shocked us and we held tightly to our dreams. We believed in the fundamental goodness of people and we trusted our own judgment. Above all, we never questioned our

---

1 Courtesy of Central Pennsylvania Convention and Visitors Bureau

morality. When we fought, we believed fervently that right was on our side.

And then tragedy struck!

When Penn State's scandal exploded, America was shocked. For the first time in modern history, the Pennsylvania State University confronted a moral catastrophe that the entire country would exploit. The "crime" was witnessed by no one. A lone graduate assistant, wandering in the coaches' locker room heard noises from the shower area, a retired coach "showering" with a teenager.

Chapter III

THE CRIME GOES PUBLIC

On the ninth day of March in the year 2001 a heinous crime befell a teenager in the football showers of the Pennsylvania State University. The crime concerned a sexual victim described as a "child" although he was a normal sized teenager. The "screams" were heard round the world, and a "cover- up" allowed the perpetrator to continue to exploit children for ten more years.

The suspicion of sexual abuse began when a young graduate assistant— wandering in the football quarters—reported "seeing" improper behavior between a retired coach and a teenager. Urged by his father, McQueary reported the incident the following day to Head Coach Joseph Paterno.

This 2001 incident was investigated and ruled poor judgment by a retired coach that did not involve sexual behavior. Almost ten years later, in 2010 the incident, now described

35

as sexual abuse, was anonymously reported to legal authorities and three weeks later, the young graduate assistant—now an assistant football coach—described a more graphic sexual encounter to a Grand Jury investigating Sandusky.

Mike McQueary[1]

The Grand Jury considered the graduate assistant, later identified as Mike McQueary, as competent. It focused on the "accurate details" that he provided of the incident, ten years after it occurred but ignored the fact that he forgot what year it happened. Thus the grand Jury report identifies the incident as taking place on March 1, 2002. After reviewing telephone logs and emails it was ascertained that the incident occurred on February 9, 2001.

Another year passed before the press release of Sandusky's indictment became the "shot heard 'round the world." Within 24 hours the entire country heard that a heinous crime had been committed—sodomy. The victim was reportedly a small boy. There was "a rush to judgment" as rumor followed rumor. The President resigned and several high-ranking Penn State officials were summarily fired before an investigation was begun.

Further factual investigation raised doubts that Mike McQueary saw anything in the shower that night, leaving the cause of the slapping noises uncertain. But Coach Jerry Sandusky was quietly suspected by members in the football circles as having a sexual problem. This could be traced back to accusations against him in 1998. Although the Local Police, State Police, the State Department of Welfare, Children and Youth Services investigated the complaint, the Centre County District Attorney concluded that "no sexual assault occurred" and no charges were brought.

Strangely, The District Attorney, Ray Gricar, disappeared without a trace in 2005. He was legally pronounced dead in 2011—although no evidence of his disappearance was ever found, so we will never know why he closed the case even though he had wire-tap evidence of Sandusky describing his assault on the teenager.

It is unclear if anyone outside Gricar's office was aware of the wire tapping, but the report of the 2001 incident faulted Penn State for a "cover-up" of this 1998 incident by the most important echelon. Added to this claim was the alleged "cover-up" of the 2001 incident (as a note no other incidents occurred on the Penn State Campus after the 2001). To the shocked world Penn State's impeccable reputation fell with shattering finality.

The story of this case, accusations of witness tampering, claims of a "cover-up" and the "rush to judgment" caused a tangled web yet unraveled. Rumors followed rumors, contradictory evidence intertwined truth and rumor, innocence fell by the wayside, sanctions mounted with frightening vindictiveness and the scandal lives on. Most damaging was the effect upon the small town of State College from which it might never recover.

The vast majority of Americans were entirely unaware that an imminent moral danger would beset this small rural town. Nor were they able to imagine the complex repercussions would follow—disaster to their favorite sport. And yet it happened! Unexpected, shocking, bizarre.

Only now do we have a glimpse into Sandusky's past. The questions that remain are: what is the full extent of his abuse and how was he able to hide his violation of boys for so many decades?

Gerald Sandusky, former defensive coordinator of the Penn State football team and founder of the Second Mile charity, was well known among prominent business and political figures. His charity was among the largest in Pennsylvania. Although the parents of victims have came forward in the past only to find unsympathetic ears among the Department of Welfare, Children and Youth Services, high school administrations, and Second Mile officers. With Penn State as the target of a cover-up, the investigation picked up speed. Whether political agendas were involved is a discussion worth having, but the truth will probably never be known.

What is known is the Grand Jury Report, which clearly focused the public's attention and emotional outrage at an alleged "cover-up" and failure to report sexual abuse of children by

Penn State officials. Factually, most abuse cases occurred outside the Penn State campus. Only a few were reported on campuses and those were subsequently investigated by Penn State authorities. The many incidents at Central Mountain High School, those at Jerry Sandusky's home, and those at other venues were not detailed or even mentioned. Failures of the Department of Welfare and Children and Youths Services were also notably absent from the report.

Tim Curley, the Athletic Director and President Spanier immediately resigned. The Penn State Football Team was at the center of the most sweeping crime known in the University's history. Over sixty years of age, Sandusky stood accused of performing over one hundred sexual acts on boys with little attention or investigation from the authorities. Sandusky pleaded innocence to all accusations. The government has collected an overwhelming number of records supported by the testimony from victims and numerous depositions—laden with inexactness, blatant lies, and false memory. The breath of scandal reached America at large in shocked disbelief. Sandusky continued to plead his innocence as the evidence against him continued to swell.

Sandusky organized The Second Mile Charity and all of his known victims were its members. No legal action was taken by those failing to notify the police, for glossing over Sandusky's suspected crimes. Supporters still question the "rush to judgment" cited by skeptical observers. They note the rapidity officials made of a loyal coach with the University for 29 years who was accused, tried and convicted with little more than sketchy public opinion. The case is, in the public mind, still inconclusive although the Grand Jury has rejected Sandusky's plea for a hearing. The sanctions and punishment continue to proliferate while support of Paterno's "innocence" strengthens with time. And the world waits in hopes that justice will prevail in the near future.

From New York to California newspapers blazed the awful facts, mixed with rumors and speculations. The town of State College was paralyzed with disbelief. Their hero, their god, Joe Paterno, was fired and died shortly afterward—he was discovered to have cancer. Argument followed argument: who knew of Coach Sandusky's crime (for many more came forth)? Did Paterno make a fatal mistake in reporting the incident to his superior instead of the Police?

The aftermath—when the world knew the story and the rumors—continued to plague the football team and the town. Prices dropped precipitously; attendance fell; businesses felt the sting of the scandal as sales dropped; reservations were cancelled; NCAA scholarships were cancelled but some later were restored; and in general the university lost its standing in the profession.

There is no question that both the town of state College and an esteemed University suffered a grave loss. Yet another important loss cannot be overlooked. Despite the confusion of fact and rumor, Joe Paterno and his legacy suffered deep permanent scars from this tragedy. Moreover, the complexity of rumors, sanctions, and political bitterness still seems to haunt Penn State—three years later.

Chapter IV

JOEPA

Once upon a time there was a boy named Joe. He was not very tall, but he was strong and well-coordinated and in love with football. He seemed destined for a career in Athletics. But there was much more—Joe was soft-spoken, gentle, highly intelligent, and self-deprecatory.

Joe Paterno in 1949 at Brown University[1]

---

1 Used with permission from the Pennsylvania State University Library Archive Collection

In short, this young Italian followed a Liberal education at Brown University and grew into, not only a national figure, but indeed, Joe became a "man for all seasons." The other side of Joe Paterno was his warmness, his generosity, and his

Joe Paterno and his family in the 1960's[1]

familial closeness. If Penn State and the Football devotees made of Joe a god, it was the product of their enormous pride in the man they nicknamed "JoePa". Joe Paterno was above all a simple man who possessed profound knowledge of the role

1 Used with permission from the Pennsylvania State University Library Archive Collection

he had to play—and did so with utmost grace and humility. On the field he was both forceful and discriminating—marching to and fro, sending "plays" to the quarterback in a critical moment, arguing with a referee when he disagreed with a decision.

The gentle Joe was—on the football field—a veritable tornado and the loyal crowd loved every minute. It was always a game that had no equal. He gave his all—not only as a coach- but as an formidable gift to his school.

He was overwhelmingly generous in endowing financial support to Penn State to enhance its already growing campus. Paterno was as concerned with the University's academic success as he was with the Athletic Program.

Joe's "gifts" to the Pennsylvania State University were generous. He was the source of an infinite number of changes in Penn State's progress toward becoming a stellar university in the United States. It is possible here—with memory on our lips—to mention only a few of his financial contributions Joe gave, not only in his capacity as Coach, but to the Academic programs of his University. He led the movement to increase the endowment to the Library, acted to raise the pay of Professors and for the

Academic scholarships, as well as to finance the construction of new buildings. Paterno 's fund-raising efforts brought in over two billion dollars that made possible the Law School, the Medical School, and a magnificent rolling campus twice the size it boasted since 1966. Yet, as a coach in the Big Ten, he was probably among the lowest paid. This, in a University whose endowment in 2007 was 1.67 billion.

Joseph Paterno came to Penn State in 1950. No one could have foreseen the enormous success he would accomplish with the rag-tag quality of its football team. Penn State was only beginning to make itself academically—competing with other state universities that enjoyed richer funding. His dream was to win the Sugar Bowl and carry his team to victory. One does not think of this quiet, ambitious, sometimes pugnacious, coach as a dreamer, but to follow his career, JoePa was ever on the success journey. He loved football and the fans loved him. The events that brought him down are not to be confused with the man he was and will be remembered as. The consensus was that Joe Paterno literally MADE State College.

The fate of Paterno has the echo of a Greek tragedy. He made one mistake and it was followed by a maelstrom of politics, false statements, and old "grudges". Ironically, Joe's reluctance to retire—except on his terms—probably contributed to his demise.

After the Sandusky scandal became public and Paterno was accused of a "cover-up", there was increasing pressure on him to retire. He declared he would retire at the end of the then current football season in 2011 which was only a few months away, but Trustees of the University ended his tenure immediately. To this day, those loyal to JoePa and those critical of his lack of action in this affair continue to disagree.

In a moment of self- deprecation Shakespeare wrote these lines:

> *When in disgrace with Fortune and men's eyes*
>
> *I all alone beweep my outcast state..........'*

So, too, felt Joseph Paterno when the voice of the Public humbled him. Turning to the team he had always loved, JoPa—still proud and self-effacing—left them with the ethical principles he had always upheld. His legacy of honesty and integrity will redeem him. This letter, to the football team, he leaves for the future as testimony.

For the last two months, at the request of the Attorney General's office, I have not discussed the specifics of my testimony regarding the pending cases. And while I will continue to honor that request, I do feel compelled to address comments made subsequent to November 9; specifically, I feel compelled to say, in no uncertain terms, that this is not a football scandal.

Let me say that again so I am not misunderstood: regardless of anyone's opinion of my actions or the actions of the handful of administration officials in this matter, the fact is nothing alleged is an indictment of football or evidence that the spectacular collections of accomplishments by dedicated student athletes should be in anyway tarnished.

Yet, over and over again, I have heard Penn State officials decrying the influence of football and have heard such ignorant comments like Penn State will no longer be a "football factory" and we are going to "start" focusing on integrity in athletics. These statements are simply unsupported by the five decades of evidence to the contrary—and succeed only in unfairly besmirching both a great University and the players and alumni of the football program who have given of themselves to help make it great.

For over 40 years young men have come to Penn State with the idea that they were going to do something different—they were coming to a place where they would be expected to compete at the highest levels of college football and challenged to get a degree. And they succeeded—during the last 45 years NO ONE has won more games while graduating more players. The men who made that commitment and who gave of themselves to help build the national reputation of what was once a regional school deserve better than to have their hard work and sacrifice dismissed as part of a "football factory," all in the interests of expediency.

Penn State is not a football factory and it is ALREADY a great University. We have world-class researchers, degree programs, and students in every discipline. Penn Staters have been pioneers in medical advancements, engineering, and in the humanities. Our graduates have gone on to change the world—even graduates with football lettermen sweaters.

That is why recent comments are so perplexing and damaging—Penn Staters know we are a world class University. We can recite with pride the ranks of our academic programs and the successes of our graduates. Penn Staters (and employers) know what we are and the quality of our education. Nothing that has been alleged in any way implicates that reputation; rather, it is only the inexplicable comments of our own administration doing so.

It must stop. This is not a football scandal and should not be treated as one. It is not an academic scandal and does not in any way tarnish the hard earned and well-deserved academic reputation of Penn State. That Penn State officials would suggest otherwise is a disservice to every one of the over 500,000 living alumni.

Forget my career in terms of my accomplishments and look at the last 40 years as I do: as the aggregate achievements of hundreds of young men working to become better people as they got an education and became better football players. Look at those men and what they have done in the world since they left Penn State and assess their contributions as an aggregate—is this a collection of jocks who did nothing but skate by at a football factory, or are these men who earned an education and built a reputation second to none as a place where academic integrity and gridiron success could thrive together?

Whatever failings that may have happened at Penn State, whatever conclusions about my or others' conduct you may wish to draw from a fair view of the allegations, it is inarguable that these actions had nothing to do with this last team or any of the hundreds of prior graduates of the "Grand Experiment."

Penn Staters across the globe should feel no shame in saying "We are...Penn State." This is a great University with one of the best academic performing football programs in major college athletics. Those are facts—and nothing that has been alleged changes them.

His final words before he died of Cancer weeks later are characteristic of the man.

"This is a tragedy. It is one of the great sorrows of my life. With the benefit of hindsight I wish I had done more."

It can be argued that Penn State power magnates were anxious for Paterno to retire—first pleading with him to retire in 2004. These requests continued until 2011, when the scandal broke—he was 85 at the time of his death—yet it remains to be seen how culpable he was in the Sandusky scandal.

Some argue he followed the rule of reporting any form of misconduct to his superior—this case to Tim Curley. Others believe Paterno's only mistake was that he did not, immediately, call in the State police or the FBI after hearing McQueary's comments about the incident. The verdict of the people is that Joe was the object of too much politics and too much reluctance to retire.

His fault was that, treated like a god, he was a mere man. His countless gifts to the University, his fair play on the field, and his basic humanity will overcome his tragic end.

It should be noted that Curley and Schulz were arraigned on charges by the Grand Jury for making false statements. Paterno was not charged. Thus, in his case, one must not condemn a figure of Paterno's stature without irrefutable truth.

Clearly, many believe, Paterno should have contacted the Police or the FBI. People will argue—as we shall see—a multitude of flaws and mistakes that made the man. What should he have done? When should he have retired? Should he have been content when his superiors told him the Sandusky issue was resolved or should he have pressed for more, even an investigation by

The Joe Paterno Statue before it and the walls were removed

the police? Until the facts are known, a shadow hovers over the name Paterno. Today, calmer heads are re-evaluating his role in what he had rightfully termed a tragedy.

Time has passed since State's moral crisis, and still it lingers in our minds, but in State College Academic and Sports lives continue with healthy vigor. Fans have returned to Football with love and enthusiasm.

The town is gradually regaining its former feeling of self-respect and nature's Spring—calm and beautiful—will echo the rebirth of Penn State's good name. A wise man once said "This too shall pass" and so we greet the future years with joy. It is one's fervent hope that Penn State shall overcome, shall regain its former reputation in athletics as well as academics. State College, hopefully, will once again raise its head with pride and confidence and honesty. Once again WE ARE PENN STATE will resound with self-esteem in the hills of Nittany country.

Chapter V

PUNISHMENTS AND SANCTIONS

When one thinks of history's notorious "Punishments" and "Sanctions", one is struck by the inhumanity people have revealed to posterity: the Spanish Inquisition, the Salem Witch Trials, the Holocaust, and—in our own recent past—the shameful evidence of the horrific treatment of slave populations after the Civil War.

So, in modern times, we find punishment and sanction continue unabated as America looks on. In the case of the Pennsylvania State University Scandal the "punishments" were plentiful, the sanctions "extreme" in severity. A "rush to judgment" has become the rule of action.

Immediately, upon publication of Sandusky's sexual exploits, a barrage of punishments and sanctions flooded Penn State . Without benefit of proof, Sandusky's guilt was accepted, ignoring the hallowed verdict: "innocent until proven guilty."

The American public saw no violation of the law and the consensus—although to be upheld in the future—was unchallenged. So disturbed was the American reaction to sexual violation of the young that this "punishment" stood firm until later supported by the Pennsylvania Supreme Court. However it took almost ten years before knowledge of Sandusky's crime became a public consideration. One does not argue Sandusky's defense here, but the carelessness which the public displayed was critical.

The Nittany Lion[1]

---

1 Courtesy of Central Pennsylvania Convention and Visitors Bureau

Such was the beginning of the Penn State search for truth. Complex distortions of the facts still continue to be heard. It is indeed difficult to weed out the truth from mere rumor, and too many innocent individuals have— as a result— suffered the dilemma.

As we shall see, many individuals long suspected Sandusky of immoral activities and "cover-ups" on many occasions. Simultaneously others lied to officials for political objectives. This resulted in inexact statements on both sides of a very complex case. America is still scratching its head in bewilderment and only the High Courts have the power to determine the truth. As the details of the scandal reached larger proportions, so too did the punishments and sanctions proliferate. Individuals as well as groups were cited by the NCAA. Almost immediately distinguished members of the football hierarchy were deemed guilty of "covering up" that which they privately knew to be suspicious or innocent. Paterno was fired together with Tim Curley and President Graham Spanier. Paterno's dismissal followed a long period when many Penn State "bigwigs" were urging him to retire. Paterno died shortly after from Cancer, but lived long enough to suffer painful shame. In his last words, he "regretted' not having done more to save his University the grim results. He termed the scandal a "tragedy".

But perhaps the severest sanctions were leveled at groups by the NCAA on the assumption that they secretly suspected Sandusky's infamous activities for ten years. Penn State University imposed sweeping penalties on the Football program, left virtually helpless with a four-year post-season ban as well as a $60 million fine. NCAA President Mark Emmert termed all this punitive. The football team was to receive a 5 year probation for any connection with the sex-abuse case. This was followed by a $13 million fine by the Big Ten Conference. More was to follow as details of Sandusky's crimes proliferated and the country became even more appalled.

More sanctions swiftly followed. Penn State was forced to renounce all of its previous victories from 1999 to 2011—including Bowl appearances. Accolades won by the players during this long period were completely eliminated with the stroke of a pen. While on probation. Penn State was not to receive football scholarships for five years. Yet it is doubtful that the Football Team had any knowledge of Sandusky's crimes despite the rapid indictment by the NCAA.

Traditionally, the NCAA is known to impose harsh punishment to football teams at Universities found to be dishonest or illegal. True, the scandal at Penn State shocked the Nation and many tended to approved the NCAA decisions of severe punishment and sanctions. Some of the Universities that came under the NCAA knife were Ohio State University for "paying" football players and "covering it up".

The NCAA also punished Miami University for giving players cash, vacations, "bounties" for injuries to opponents. Coaches knew all of these practices. Other colleges and universities suffered a similar punishment. They include West Virginia, Florida State, Maryland, Texas A&M, Kentucky, Stanford, Alabama and Cornell.

Punishments were severe: Scholarships were removed. Fines in the millions were levied. Many teams were placed on probation, sweeping penalties were inflicted on teams. Nothing compared with the punishments and sanctions Penn State suffered, but this was perhaps the first NCAA sanctions' case in which none of the players were involved in the scandal.

Only the head coach and the athletic director were involved. As we shall see, there was a strong feeling in the public mind that the Penn

State University Football Team was innocent of any knowledge of either Sandusky's activities or the "cover-up" that followed.

Continual punishment and sanctions serve a major objective—that of preventing immoral or questionable behavior on the part of a group or individual. Or it may well serve to perpetuate in one's National memory a horrendous human act. This is precisely what the Penn State multiplication of punishments and sanctions has produced in this tragic affair.

Others argue that NCAA sanctions are used to tightly control the members as well as to protect the billions in revenue earned by the NCAA. These profits accrue from games, endorsements and other marketing materials. Without strict discipline, there is fear that players may rebel and seek wages and royalties.

Currently, many skilled players seek professional sports contracts, even directly out of high school because of the vast financial rewards. College education, once considered essential, is being bypassed or shortened to compete for multi-million dollar salaries of professional sports.

In addition to the NCAA punishments, the University paid twenty-six people $59.7 million to settle Sandusky's sex abuse claims. Many questions yet remain.

Chapter VI

THE PUBLIC SPEAKS OUT

Upon the heels of the Penn State Scandal, public opinion quickened. It seemed as if the American public rapidly knew all the truth and was ready to be heard. This was a gross mistake. The truth was shot through with rumor, inexactness, lies, past grudges, and—most detrimental—the wide-spread "cover-up." Judgment without basis, condemnation without proof, defense without knowledge was common. All have clashed in the arena of public opinion. Today, until the Higher Courts have made definitive decisions, and the truth be known, the differences of opinion will prevail.

In seeking the facts of the case, one is hampered by the intense emotion that accompany individual opinions and "first class testimony." Each is cluttered with misconception, and lies, and objectivity is the victim. This could be termed the "Battle of the Public." A mere illustration of this "battle" reveals several impediments to the

Truth. A variety of concerned opinions serve to demonstrate this complexity.

Mike McQueary, former quarterback of the Nittany Lions confessed to a Grand Jury in 2011 that he told to his father and Joe Paterno he saw Jerry Sandusky "sexually abuse a young child" in the shower of the Football Athletic quarters. Subsequently, this proved to be part of a tissue of lies. What he did experience was noises emanating from a shower stall occupied by a teenager he did not recognize and a retired coach. He did NOT report immediately to his superior, Joe Paterno, but claims he lived in fear of the exposure of his own "secret."

Mike McQueary confessed to a friend that he was a sex-abused child and admitted he had been a victim, but he repeated this "fable" later. Differing sworn statements about the incidents provided by Mike McQueary are claimed to exist because the trauma of his own abuse prevents him, at times, of describing the incident in detail. Quite possibly, he was never abused but lied to gain sympathy.

Mike McQueary also has a $4 million dollar lawsuit against Penn State, claiming his job was terminated solely because he was a whistle blower. That case is still moving through the court system. Behind closed doors, he again told the players what he had never before disclosed. One player said, "It was heartbreaking for all of us. We were not sure who to believe." Thus, the "whisle blower" made his last stand.

An irate resident of State College believes that the entire "cover-up" was created by Joe Paterno in an effort to secure his very large pay check and treasure house of Ego! From his perspective, Joe's attachment to Sandusky was his "Achilles Heel," preventing him from seeing the truth.

Editorial comment: This accusation has no basis in fact.

One angry graduate student fervently believes in Joe's innocence of any connection with a "conspiracy of silence". Paterno's predominant personal goal in life happened on the football field. His devotion and generosity and humane treatment to his team players preclude the possibility of moral indictment. He was a hero for all seasons.

An astute member of the public noted this: the NCAA punished Penn State heavily while profiting in the millions. They did revoke the wins and titles earned, and maybe the $60 million fine was to take away Penn State's profits from those games. Taking away scholarships and not allowing Penn State to play bowl games hurt the team's future.

BUT, the NCAA made many millions of profits on those games as well and profited many more millions on player and team promotions (players are not paid for sponsorships). Penn State made some profit on items sold at the University, but the NCAA was the big financial winner.

Since the games were wiped away and since Penn State paid their "profits" back to the NCAA, why does the NCAA get to keep the hundreds of millions they made in profits on those games and the $60 million fine? Shouldn't they take this "unholy" profit and give it to a charity serving child abuse?

A disillusioned Collegian points to the attitude toward Joe's prestige as a hero—more exactly—as a god who could know the law and deliberately ignore it. To the fans who worshipped Paterno, he could do no wrong—nor heed a horrendous activity that might ruin his own spectacular career.

Another individual, commenting on Sandusky's twenty-nine years as a loyal and competent coach to the football team, felt that dismissing him as a "sexual predator" in 1998 was illegal and disloyal, despite his creation of The Second Mile to "save" young boys.

The accusations, the punishment, and the sanctions multiplied daily and the State College public watched their idols fall into ruin. The NCAA levied punishment and sanctions on the Penn State Football team; high-ranking officials were fired, including Penn State's President Spanier and the University fell from grace overnight. Such was the judgment of the Public before any defense was forthcoming."

Other accusations were made as the Public voice supported the judgment attacking such power moguls as the NCAA, Governor Tom Corbett, Schultz, and Curley. Fragments of their opinions can be cited here.

An airplane was rented to promote the removal of a statue of Joe Paterno that had been constructed in his honor. Today, that memorial remains hidden from view in some unknown storage bin—reminding students of Paterno's shame.

But repeatedly, the condemnation centers on the primary "Sins"—Money and Ego, comments one observer. To lose either would be "death'" to every high-ranking member of Penn

State's ruling class. Paterno refused to retire under pressure and Sandusky—though retired—was still a presence ten years later.

And then there was the Public voice claiming "innocence" for ALL accused of moral or political advancement—denying a "cover-up" and declaring that The Second Mile was a benevolent Society.

As disgusting as Sandusky's actions are, it is an illness and many more people suffer from the same disease. These people need serious help that I believe has no cure, comments one resident.

A disillusioned fan concluded "Football is the "Hall of Shame."

Clearly, the bitterness, the disappointment, the anger, and the confusion among the Public at large has complicated the search for truth in this historic affair. Members of the Public expressed their "gut" reactions without seeking facts, and the result was often useless. Yet, the higher courts and The Board of Trustees of The Pennsylvania State University will perhaps make the final judgment.

Although it was impossible to find a consensus in this or countless numbers of public voices, the most common theme was to state the motives as "money and self-esteem." Listen to this voice: This—the power that money and prestige has over people...the Grand Jury report indicates a large number of eyewitnesses who all told someone about the incidents they witnessed but nobody at the State College Police Department or Penn State was willing to take the case seriously because of the scandal it would erupt.,.JoePa let it sit for 10 years.

And there were the "Defenders."

One angry fan reminded us that Sandusky was an excellent defense coach for 29 years and then was "dumped" solely on the basis of vicious gossip.

The "humane" Sandusky, says another, was interested mainly in helping poor young boys through The Second Mile.

Defending Paterno's important role in Penn State's success, one irate fan cited the several ways Paterno raised the profile not only of the Penn State football program but of the University as well.

Another voice declared it was unconscionable to hold Joe Paterno responsible either for the actions of a sex maniac or for the "cover-up" that followed. Joe was an honest, dependable, loyal man. His enemies—envious of his public reputation—shamed him into stating that he wished he had done more. Look at the record of unselfish acts he performed for Penn State, how many wonderful advances he alone could claim.

Not only was he a successful Coach but a proud supporter of the University's Academic reputation. Another lifelong resident of State College, angry at the slander hurled at Paterno, reminds the public that "Paterno was idolized by his team, the fans, the Alumni for the role he played in helping Penn State to build a Law School, a Medical School, offer Scholarships enrich the Library and add new buildings."

It has been generally accepted, one State College resident noted, that the Penn State Football Team was totally unaware of the sex violations Sandusky stood accused of. Yet, when the news broke and the "punishments and sanctions given, the Pennsylvania State University Football team was fined 60 million dollars and several sanctions. It is not clear whether these have been reversed.

Thus, we can conclude that many innocent people were judged by "popular" concurrence to be guilty of either "cover-up", knowledge of the law, or personal, political. or financial motives.

Another writes, "I have read the 23 page testimony to the Grand Jury and Sandusky should have been in jail for over 12 years now. There are MANY to blame for this cover-up...."

The people who witnessed the abuse, reported it years ago. Did they not feel the need to follow up with that? Were they so concerned about their jobs that they just let it go?

It's too bad the University waited until this horrific story went public to hold an investigation.

It's a shame that JoePa's long and illustrious career should end on such a note. A whole life of hard work destroyed by a subordinate's scandal.

From even a small sampling it is obvious that the Public—at large—is incapable of making a clear decision in this historic case. Too many testify without sufficient evidence; too many have emotional reasons to judge objectively. The Salem Witch Trials, the Spanish Inquisition, the discrimination of native American Indians in the birth of this country were as guilty of erroneous "decisions." Now, in modern times, the Public Voice is not only confused. It is largely uninformed. Only a higher authority—like the

Grand Jury of Pennsylvania—or a well-researched body of jurors will place blame or innocence on those, under a cloud, with justice.

Chapter VII

THE BOARD OF TRUSTEES

The highest ruling body in all universities is the prestigious Board of Trustees. It establishes University policy, approves professorial hiring, promotion and, in some cases, professorial "reward." In the case of The Pennsylvania State University, it shares responsibilities and rules of behavior. The Board of Trustees is, in general conservative, stern in upholding its standard and well-respected for its seriousness and objectivity. It holds, as its responsibility the good name of the University and is not beholden to other highly-placed officials.

However, the Board claims it was not informed of the 1998 investigation or the 2001 abuse claims. The conspiracy of silence was able to exclude the Board of Sandusky's activities. Given the 1998 investigation involving campus police, state police, the Center County Attorney, the Second Mile organization, The State Department of Welfare, Children and Youths Services, the president and vice president of Penn State and political leaders, one can only wonder why none of the 32 member board had knowledge of the incident. The Board failed to exercise its oversight and reasonable inquiry responsibilities for both the 1998 and the 2001 incidents. It reportedly learned of the incidents after ten years had elapsed and the affair was publicized nationwide.

As one would expect, the Board of Trustees played a significant role in the crisis that shook the very foundations of The Pennsylvania State University. To that end, they commissioned a special investigative counsel headed by Louis Freeh to analyze claims of a "cover-up" and review the circumstances that permitted the abuse to occur. Their "findings" , The Freeh Report, would be so convincing that the Board would find it imperative to severely impose upon Penn State unimpeachable regulations.

The Policies and Procedures decreed by the Board were, subsequently, harsh and unambiguous. They included risk and reporting misconduct, responsibilities and operations. The Board of Trustees would work closely with the Athletic Department and the University Police. In addition, the Board of Trustee redesigned its committees adding a new focus to audit, risk, legal and compliance. While the Board members were "deeply ashamed" by the findings of the Freeh Report and many notable groups called for resignations, no trustee resigned.

Sadly, in 2004 the Board became concerned about their role in "rubber-stamping" University decisions. Perhaps this concern was driven by the Sarbanes-Oxley Act which established new levels of compliance, accountability and best practices throughout public companies, some of which were represented by trustees.

They consulted with an outside law firm to bring sweeping changes to the responsibilities and operations of the Board of Trustees. Their goal, as noted on a meeting memo was to "enable the trustees to act in the best interest of the university, the administration and the various constituencies we represent." A number of significant changes to the university's by-laws, giving the board ultimate authority for personnel decisions was also made.

None of these amendments were voted on by the Board. The Freeh Report did not discuss these proposed changes or why none were adopted. They could have made a significant difference in the culture possibly avoiding the damages of the Sandusky scandal.

Chapter VIII

HAPPY VALLEY

Nestled in the folds of Nittany and Tussy Mountains—far from the "madding crowd"— lies the town of State College, proud home of The Pennsylvania State University. True to its beginnings as a rural village, State College still has no railroad stop, a modest airfield, and few

Downtown[1]

---

1 Copyright 2014 - Kaye Productions

luxury hotels. Yet, in many respects it is modern, and up-to-date in its "living" aspects. The private homes are luxurious; the apartments large and comfortable, and the movie houses timely. In winter, the roads are cleared of snow and in summer, air-conditioning is universal.

Happy Valley has been successful in becoming the third safest borough in the United States and attracts many residents to its limited area. In addition Happy Valley has been considered the third best college town in the United States.

In the beginning this isolated village, born in 1855, was largely an agricultural region, known as The Farmers' High School of Pennsylvania. Since, its population has reached over 104.000 residents. Today, it is known officially as the municipal borough of State College. Happy Valley largely owes its progress to the phenomenal growth of The State University of Pennsylvania and the numerous scientific Research Laboratories within its boundaries. In 1976, State College adopted a home-rule charter and thereafter became a borough. Apart from its reputation as a major "Football" centre, it hosts a seasonal Festival of the Arts—attracting tourists from East and West—and numerous theatrical performances year round.

State College is a home-rule municipality in Centre County in the State of Pennsylvania. In 2010 the borough population grew from 40,000 to its present number. The community is a "college town dominated economically and demographically in keeping with the rising growth of Penn State's campus. Happy Valley is an affectionate nick-name for this unique town.

Clearly, a "division" exists between the University and State College- often referred to as "The Thin Blue Line." This results at times in conflicts between "townies" and University faculty. The only crisis came when the University changed its name, but State College retained its original identity. A walk in Happy Valley reveals its emphasis on familiar, village values. Who can forget one's frequent dinners at The Tavern, or shopping in The Charles Shop, or lunching at The Autoport or The Corner Room of The State College Hotel, or buying Christmas gifts at Kranich's Jeweler, or checking out books from the Schlow Library at the corner of Allen Street? How the taste buds remember the cinnamon rolls—hot off the grille- from the Diner!

The Corner Room[1]

The Corner at Allen Street and College Avenue will always be the focal meeting place— where town meets University, where friends meet friends. Just a few steps away is the Chinese Restaurant, and the Coffee Shop for "Espresso ."

---

1 Courtesy of Central Pennsylvania Convention and Visitors Bureau

"Dinner" at the creamery[1]

Penn State's claim to fond memory is the Creamery on campus where home bound football fans still savor the taste of the best ice cream in the State. All the "stops" one makes in Happy Valley only accentuate the interdependence of Town and Gown. Each shares its popularity with the other for despite their differences or disagreements, they share the other's destiny. The success of Paterno's football team is reflected in Happy Valley's economy. Similarly a scandal on campus will weigh heavily on State College.

Great pain has no ending. Whether caused by the death of a loved one or the fall into ignomy

---

or simply the "happening" in our presence or the change from pride and respect to contempt or scorn, the pain lives on as if with a life of its own. The events surrounding the Sandusky Scandal seem—on the surface—to have abated. We shall hear of a new future—economically, psychologically, and emotionally—but beneath the brave exterior, Happy Valley is still licking its wounds. The country has yet to understand or forget the crime, and the Press and the on-going litigation keep gossip alive. Given the evidence that will enforce our stubborn memories to be reminded of the disgrace, the contempt, and the pain we will carry on and hope that the history of this crime "will pass….."

And so it happened in 2011 when Penn State suffered its first major crisis. Happy Valley—who had never known the name "Sandusky"—suddenly experienced shame and guilt throughout the entire Nation.

It is common knowledge that the chief emotional bond between Penn State and Happy Valley has been Football. With the success of Head Coach Joseph Paterno, this hitherto unknown sport had grown into a National phenomenon—a member of the Big Ten, two trips to the Rose Bowl and the unqualified love of countless fans.

Though the monument of JoePa lies hidden on Campus soil, he will retain the stature of a god. Residents of Happy Valley will always defend his role in the Sandusky Scandal and an equal number will censure him for all time. The impact of that event will have a lasting effect upon State College, symbolized by Paterno's legacy.

The horizon darkened ominously for State College when the "McQueary" confession exploded on the tranquil world of Centre County. Yet, Penn State "fame" will always be equated with Joe Paterno whose grave in Spring Creek Cemetery is covered with loving mementos of his unforgettable success in his Football career and especially his generosity in Academic matters. In addition, he supported the Penn State Law School, the Penn State Medical School as well as countless numbers of scholarships and new buildings.

It is difficult to assess the impact Penn State's Scandal has had on the town itself. As complex as that affair became—sweeping like wildfire across the country—more and more people pointed blame; more and more claimed to have been "witnesses" to the Sandusky crime. Perhaps, the most damaging element was the "cult of silence" taken by the highest University authorities in their desperate effort to save the good name of the University.

Happy Valley was as divided in its opinions as the University. To this day, investigators do not possess the unvarnished truth and so the Scandal lives on.

Of significant importance is the question: "Given the close relationship of Town and Gown, has State College suffered economically, psychologically, and emotionally from the Sandusky Scandal and the inevitable, complex, and endless results of that misfortune?" Many crucial questions are immediately raised. Since Football season occurred in 2001 precisely when Michael McQueary reported what he saw to Paterno (since negated), what has been the lasting effect on Happy Valley?

State College, stunned by the heinous nature of the "crime," reacted almost immediately to the news. Of such enormity was the effect upon townspeople that disbelief was universal. The pain and anger that followed can hardly be described. The mere idea of inflicting "sex crime" on young children was unbearable, and the "cover-up" contemptible. Again, the destiny of Happy Valley was inextricably bound to that of Penn State.

There is no question that more than 5000 football fans boycotted Penn State Football games in the Fall of 2011 once the scandal became universally known. The maelstrom of trials, punishments, and sanctions became popular knowledge. The revulsion felt in Happy Valley was equaled only by the disclosure by University officials of the "cult of silence" or "cover-up" that postponed the legal investigation. State College was as confused by rumor, lies, and contradictory testimony as the rest of the country. And the result was felt by all of Centre County.

If the Football Scandal kept fans away, hotels suffered the consequences. Restaurants lacked the evening crowds. Motels lost business they had waited to fill a year earlier. Clothing stores—filled with Penn State memorabilia waited unsuccessfully for business. Fans who shopped yearly in Allen Street never appeared. A pall hung over an otherwise healthy town because of the rash of malignant publicity that is still in process of investigation by Federal authorities.

Any study of the economic health of a region will encounter fluctuations—rises and falls—that reflect the normal changes of the country as a whole. It is only when long established businesses close their doors at an alarming rate and when the public is beset with rumor and notoriety that the reputation of a public haunt plummets. One cannot assume that the Sandusky Scandal caused the failure of all the establishments that closed shop in Happy Valley. Too many felt the sting of boycott. Roughly seventeen businesses shut their doors in the past few years, even as new enterprises fought to establish economic roots and struggled to offset the lingering blight of a bad press nationally AND THE PERRENIAL SKEPTICS.

Among those enterprises that suffered closure were restaurants, beauty parlors, bookstores, bars, and Penn State memorabilia/clothing stores. The most notable were Mr. Charles, Neebo, The Rag and Bone Shop, Flash Décor, Lipstick, Duo, The Mad Hatter, Quiznos, Attic, Iuphoria, Fresh Harvest Café, Penn State Sub Shop, Philly Pretzel, and Happy Valley Freeze. The closing of Mr. Charles, a high fashion Women's shop, was a shock to long-term residents who recall the success it sustained for many years. They will always remember the halcyon days when Mr. Charles was the style-setter of Happy Valley.

Thus, the economic conditions in Happy Valley suffered a down-turn that it is now struggling to ameliorate.

And the residents of Happy valley? They are mixed in their opinions. Some place blame only on Sandusky's activities over a ten year period despite frequent warnings. Some refuse to cite Joe Paterno for any infringement of the rules in reporting crimes. Some blame ALL who knew the truth of a "conspiracy of silence" to shield themselves and The Pennsylvania State University. However noble their intentions, the outcome was nearly disastrous for both Penn State and State College.

State College made its opinions public and fraught with emotion. This was their home and their lives were given to it—Happy Valley would not be the victim of a bad press or a rumor factory. Nonetheless, the proliferation of punishments, sanctions imposed by NCAA authorities confused many residents. Some—who perhaps lived in State College for years—picked up stakes and left.

The most vocal residents expressed themselves to several public media—a mere segment that can be reproduced here. Listen to the voices of state Collegians. Most responded to the wide coverage with which they disagreed. Listen to their voices:

Do you realize the media is not the court of the land. No court has heard this case of "blame" yet….He (Sandusky) was cleared by three government agencies of the 1998 incident. He was an incredibly respected man whose charity, whose charity, boasted helping 100,000 kids.

I do not think most people realize that there is absolutely no real evidence against Paterno or anyone at PSU (except Sandusky). People assume they were fired because they were guilty but no one really knows what happened in 2011. The only available information was a Grand Jury Report which was completely one-sided, and we now know it was full of inaccuracies. No one was given a chance to defend themselves. The board of Trustees was overcome by pressure from the media, demands from politicians and the public's outrage over the Grand Jury press release. Firing people seemed their only recourse.

Only Paterno was fired. Spanier resigned as President. Schultz, the Athletic Director, retired. Curley was placed on administrative leave. Curley and Schultz testified that McQueary only told them it was horseplay, a question of their honesty or McQueary's credibility.

Paterno was not charged with a crime and had already promised to retire at the end of the season, two months away. Yet he was fired rather than placed on administrative leave.

After the truth and proper perspective are finally gained concerning this criminal incident, JoePa's memory will most likely be memorialized as it already is on Campus with the Library and the Museum additions. The Paterno Family continues to fight for its Patriarch's legacy. Its lawsuit against the NCAA moves forward.

The only divide in the Community is over the actions of the old guard Board of Trustees, hell bent on retaining their power. As the rest of us watched in shock, they make repeated failures in the wake of their knowledge of Sandusky's pending indictment.

Some express their wrath on Sandusky. An incensed resident wrote:

> *"Assuming Sandusky is guilty based on the Grand Jury Report, the trial testimony, and Sandusky's own statements—it certainly appears that way—I hope he burns in eternal Hell. Death would be too good for him."*

Despite the range of opinions fraught with emotion, if not often truth, many of these views expressed here do not reflect the damages suffered.

Perhaps the most damning response came from a long-time resident of State College taking Paterno to task. It accuses JoePa of many flaws that the more loyal deny.

> "I believe Paterno felt himself a God and did not want to retire at 85. He loved his job along with the great wealth and the prestige it brought him. He was a big fish in a little pond and was a victim of money and ego... Sandusky was his Achilles Heel. And he could not bring Sandusky down...He could not bring Penn State down—it was his Empire. He refused the pressures to retire despite urging from above".

It is clear that Joe Paterno was more favorably judged by the Happy Valley residents than censured. Today, the image of an honest, generous humble man seems to be the predominant view. State College was hurt economically, psychologically, and emotionally and one never can predict when the Sandusky Scandal will fade into the past.

While almost three years have passed since the Sandusky scandal exploded, its lingering effects are evident in discussions with shop owners, residents, even the local police force. Sales are down, tax revenues are down, and hence services are at their lowest level since 2010.

Reduced sales means reduced purchases and thus higher purchasing costs as volume is key in purchasing. While some made drastic cutbacks to survive, others were unable to continue under the economic stress.

Chapter IX

HAPPY VALLEY TODAY

Three years have slipped by since Happy Valley was struck by the infamous scandal that hovered over its existence. There was fear that its once heralded reputation, after decades of growth and prosperity, would sink into dust. Nonetheless, State College has made a remarkable recovery. The rumors are mere echoes; the "heroes" are gone; the "conspiracy of silence" is dismantled. Happy Valley—though injured—reveals signs of healthy restitution. Spring is imminent and the Football players will soon be on the field gearing up for the Blue-White Game.

We always knew that State College's destiny was an integral part of Penn State University's life, and we prayed to weather the storm and await the calm and hope that both Town and Gown learn from past events.

Today, Happy Valley is an icon for progress in the State of Pennsylvania. Economically, psychologically , and socially the State has made enormous strides since the end of the great Scandal.

Happy Valley is back! Today one sees changes to her landscape in every direction. The current motif is modernism combined with spaciousness. The central thoroughfare, Atherton Street, has been enlarged and widened—cutting across State College North and South. As a result, builders have joined this renovation by constructing high-rise buildings to attract new businesses. Gone are the shabby trailer parks that cluttered North Atherton for decades. New restaurants, motels, coffee shops, and bars are yet in the future along North Atherton.

In the center of the borough, increased building activity is currently underway.

Yet, pain has no "finale". Nonetheless, the events surrounding the Sandusky Scandal seem— on the surface—to have abated. We hear of a new economic surge in State College. We know of new economic businesses... The strength of new business and investment has amazingly reinforced the substructure of Happy Valley's future. Today, State College is reborn. More than one hundred new businesses have been established in Happy Valley as buildings rise skyward to accommodate them. The variety is almost endless as the borough increases its offerings. Today, State College is its assuming traditional destiny.

It is clear that Happy Valley has overcome its crisis that so threatened a town whose experience had little to do with this catastrophe. A sample of the rich variety of businesses continually establishing in Centre County is ample proof that sound economic success is the future for Happy Valley and hopefully for The Pennsylvania State University.

The great variety of new businesses is amazing! Not merely numbers but types of offerings tempt the contemporary buyers. Among the "New" are regional restaurants, book stores, bike shops, barber shops and beauty parlors, florists, menswear, physical fitness gyms, automobile parts, and wine shops. By far, the greatest and most popular are the restaurants which compete favorably with big city offerings.

A sampling of some of Happy Valley's thriving businesses are The Mountain View Country Club, Foredathes Book Shop, Quaker Steak, Dickey's Barbecue Pit, Kamrai Thai and Sushi House. Your Gym Closet, Happy Valley Vineyard and Winery,Golden Ladle, Ni Hao Asian Cuisine, Gap, Men's Warehouse. Samantha

Doan's Bakery, Gardners Candies, Anytime fitness and Mcalisters Deli. These suggest only a few of the "hundred" newly registered businesses.

If there is any doubt that Happy Valley has undergone an incredible rebirth, one has only to note the increasing number of former State College youngsters who—now as retirees—have returned to enjoy "the calm after the storm."

Together with the new are the old beloved haunts. The Tavern is still Number One for dinner, reminding us of its beginnings with pictures of its origins as well as offering us its succulent fare. The Waffle Shop is busy from dawn to sundown and the Chinese Restaurant, The Deli, the Corner Room, Gamble's Mill, and the Olive Garden are all doing a lively business. Motels are booking for the 2014 Football season and Happy Valley is again, economically sound. But State College seems to herald a substantially larger role as Penn State tries to forget the past and plans its future—to insure Joe Paterno's legacy and mostly his pride.

Added to all this, private home building is covering the fringes of the once-rural landscape. Many former children—now near retirement—

are returning to build their "dream" homes, fulfilling the notion that "You can go home again."

Perhaps the most exciting and popular single event of each year is the Pennsylvania Festival of the Arts. Its beginnings grew from a small display and sidewalk sales of locally crafted paintings and inexpensive jewelry to the present varied exhibitions. Over the years it expanded to attract visitors from central State College and nearby states.

Crowd at the Arts Festival[1]

Beginning, initially, from the University Library, the Festival lines the Mall to College Avenue and Allen Street. The event runs 4 days mid-summer, exhibits and sells paintings, sculpture, handmade knitwear, silver and gold

1 Courtesy of Central Pennsylvania Convention and Visitors Bureau

jewelry, and nationally recognized Arts. Each year new exhibits make their appearance and the attendance grows. At least 125,000 visitors are expected to arrive for this years festival.

In addition to the sidewalk displays, exhibits are housed inside University buildings. Together with Art, activity abounds with productions of plays, dance, sculpture, music and theatre performances.

In an ambitious enterprise the Pennsylvania Festival of the Arts will ever testify to the Sisterhood of Town and Gown.

First Night[1]

As prosperity increases—apart from the bitter memories of the Scandal—the cultural life

---

1 Courtesy of Central Pennsylvania Convention and Visitors Bureau

of Happy Valley grows. The museums are richly endowed. Dance recitals are regularly offered. Musical concerts fill the Bryce Jordan Center. Theatres visit all year round and upcoming Centre County regional shows perform regularly.

Happy Valley, once a rural village and merely a part of Penn State today is independent, culturally rich, and standing tall as an American icon.

EPILOGUE

In the year 2011 tragedy of an infamous magnitude struck one of America's finest institutions. The Pennsylvania State University—pride of State College, model of learning in many academic disciplines, epitome of good sportsmanship—Penn State fell to an ignominious low within twenty-four hours, as the world was stunned by the scandal that unfolded. It was, indeed, a Greek tragedy in the modern sense. There is no blaming, no indictment of a town gone haywire over football, no punishment for hubris or challenge of the gods. There are only the sorry facts, the mistakes, and the acts of one demented human being.

Yet, it lingers in our minds, in State College Academics and Sports with a persistent vigor. Fans have begun to return to Football gradually with love and enthusiasm. The town is slowly regaining its former feeling of self-respect, calm and beauty—all will echo the rebirth of Penn State's good name. A wise man once said "This too shall pass", and so we greet the future years with confidence. Penn State shall overcome, shall regain its former reputation in Athletics as well as Academics. State College will once again raise its head with pride and honesty. Once again WE ARE PENN STATE! will resound with self-esteem in the hills of Nittany country.

Hints of Spring are in the air—the early Forsythia are crowding the Campus, the scent of Lilac perfumes the Mall. Hope cancels out despair. The Pennsylvania State University is on its way back!

Joe's words while he lay waiting to die were: "Just get the truth. I have confidence. Make sure the truth comes out."

TIME LINE

DATE	DESCRIPTION
Feb. 22, 1855	Farmers High School founded
1875	Name changed to Pennsylvania State College
1922	Formation of Graduate School
1950	Joe Pattern hired as assistant coach
Apr. 20, 1952	National Educational television broadcasting founded at Penn State— Later to become the Public Broadcasting Service, PBS
1953	University status granted
1966	Joe Paterno becomes head coach of the "Nittany Lions"

1967	Penn State expands by adding a medical school
1968	Penn State Nittany Lions go undefeated in regular season
1969	Sandusky joins the Penn State coaching staff
1969	Penn State Nittany Lions go undefeated in regular season
1977	Sandusky founds The Second Mile charity
1982	Penn State wins national football championship
1986	Penn State wins national football championship
1989	Dickinson Law School becomes part of Penn State
June 1995	Tom Corbett appointed Attorney General of Pennsylvania—the previous Attorney General, Ernie Preate, resigned after being found guilty of mail fraud
May 3, 1998	Sandusky showers with teenager at Penn State

May 4, 1998	Mother of child calls Penn State police and accuses Sandusky of giving her son a bear hold while naked in the shower
May 4, 1998	Penn State police notify Children and Youth Services about the complaint
May 4, 1998	Penn State police notify Centre County District Attorney's office
May 5, 1998	State Department of Public Welfare notifies Penn State police that they too are investigating
May 9, 1998	"Psychologist" hired by Children and Youth Services reports that Sandusky does not fit the profile of a pedophile
May 11, 1998	Mother calls Penn State police again concerned about a recent call from Sandusky for her son

May 13, 1998	Penn State police inform Centre County District Attorney's Office
May 1998	Centre County District Attorney, Ray Gricar decides there is not sufficient evidence to accuse Sandusky
Jun. 1, 1998	Case against Sandusky is closed
1999	Sandusky retires as defensive coordinated at Penn State
Feb. 9, 2001	Sandusky showers with teenager and is discovered by graduate assistant Mike McQueary
Feb. 9, 2001	McQueary reports incident to his father and a family friend, a well know doctor neither of whom interpret McQueary's description as a sexual encounter— McQueary does not think a crime was committed
Feb. 10, 2001	At his father's insistence, McQueary reports the incident, described as

	horseplay, to his boss Joe Paterno
Feb. 11, 2001	Joe Paterno reports the incident to his boss, Athletic director Tim Curley and Executive Vice President, and head of the Penn State Police, Gary Schultz
Feb. 12, 2001	President Graham Spanier is informed
Feb. 25, 2001	Spanier, Shultz and Curley meet to address incident and determine a plan of action
Mar. 19, 2001	The Second Miles is notified and Sandusky is told to no longer bring any youths to the locker room—as a note Sandusky does not bring any more boys to Penn State locker rooms
Mar. 1, 2002	Date that McQueary provides Grand Jury for the incident— later we learn that February 9, 2001 is the correct date

Jan. 2004	Tom Corbett sworn in as Attorney General of Pennsylvania
Nov. 2004	Joe Paterno is asked to retire by the Board of Trustees
Nov. 2004	The Penn State Board of Trustees propose sweeping reforms to strengthen their oversight powers at the University—however, the proposal is never voted upon
Apr. 15, 2005	Ray Gricar, Centre County District Attorney, disappears and never is found i
Jun. 2005	The destroyed hard drive from Ray Gricar's laptop is found in the Susquehanna River
July 2006	Investigators announce that 13 months earlier, Ray Gricar was seen with a mystery women at an antique mall on the day he disappeared—the mystery women was never identified

Nov. 2008	"Victim 1" reports to police that Sandusky had assaulted him
Mar. 2009	Pennsylvania Attorney General Tom Corbett begins a Grand Jury to investigate the claim against Sandusky— one investigator is assigned to the case
2010	Tom Corbett campaigns for governor
2010	Past and present Board members of Second Mile donate over $200,000 to Corbett's campaign for governor
Nov. 2010	Centre County District Attorney receives anonymous email regarding 2001 incident in the Penn State shower along with McQueary's name
Dec. 14, 2010	Grand Jury interviews McQueary who describes the incident in great detail and claims inaccurately that

it occurred on March 1, 2002—McQueary testimony now clearly describes sexual activity

Jan. 11, 2011	Tom Corbett sworn in as Governor of Pennsylvania
Jan. 12, 2011	Paterno, Curley and Schultz testify before Grand Jury
Mar. 8, 2011	Governor Corbet proposes sweeping budget cuts for higher education, 60% cut to Penn State
Mar. 9, 2011	Spanier hold press conference blasting the budget cuts
Apr. 2011	Grand Jury subpoenas Jack Raykovitz, President of the Second Mile to testify
Jul. 2011	Grand Jury files secret contempt motion against The Second Mile
Nov. 2011	Seven investigators are assigned to Sandusky Grand Jury
Nov. 4, 2011	Sandusky charged with 40 counts of child abuse

Nov. 5, 2011	Press release of Sandusky charges is published
Nov. 8, 2011	Penn State Board of Trustees meet in a conference call to express outrage and form an investigation committee
Nov. 9, 2011	Penn State Board of Trustees meet—Governor Corbett, takes part in the meeting and urges other members to fire Paterno
Nov. 9, 2011	Spanier resigns
Nov. 9, 2011	Paterno who reportedly refused to retire is fired by a telephone call
Nov. 11, 2011	Second Mile removes names of board members/staff from website
Nov. 11, 2011	Grand Jury Report is released and contrary to McQueary's original testimony, clearly defines sodomy as the act he witnessed.
Nov. 11, 2011	Governor Corbett announces investigation into Sandusky's Second Mile Charity

Nov. 14, 2011	The president and CEO if The Second Mile steps down
Nov. 21, 2011	Penn State hires law firm Freeh Sporkin & Sullivan LLP for $6.5 million to investigate Penn State involvement and to recommend actions
Dec. 7, 2011	Sandusky is arrested
Dec. 16, 2011	Curley and Schultz are charged with perjury, their trials are still to come. Joe Paterno is not charged
Jan. 22, 2012	Joe Paterno dies
May 25, 2012	Second Mile announces plans to close and transfer programs to a Texas non-profit
Jun. 11, 2012	Sandusky trial starts
Jun. 13, 2012	Mike McQueary takes the stand and testifies that he clearly witnessed a sex act that Sandusky performed on a boy

Jun. 22, 2012	Sandusky is found guilty of 45 of the 48 counts
Jul. 12, 2012	The infamous Freeh Report is released claiming a cover-up by Penn State officials, including coach Joe Paterno
Jul. 22, 2012	Penn State learns of severe punishment and sanctions from the NCAA
Jul. 22, 2012	Joe Paterno statue is removed and the remaining monument destroyed outside Beaver Stadium
Oct. 9, 2012	Sandusky sentenced to 30 to 60 years in prison
Jan. 7, 2014	Original trial date for Tim Curley, Gary Schultz and Graham Spanier on perjury charges related to the Sandusky sex abuse incidents—now delayed indefinitely
2014	Mike McQueary awaits court date for his $4 million whistle blower suit against Penn State